HOW TO CAPTURE THE POWER

OF POSITIVE ENERGY

DR. NASSER AFIFY

2019

TABLE OF CONTENTS

INTRODUCTION

Energy" in physics means some very specific things. For example, kinetic energy of an object having a mass m and a velocity v is given by $1/2 \, mv^2$. There are other kinds of energy in physics: gravitational potential energy, electromagnetic potential energy, thermal energy, etc. These are also defined by various formulas involving measurable characteristics of a physical system. The thing that makes energy a useful concept is that it's "conserved." That means that when you compute the total energy of a thing when you add up all its kinetic energy, potential energy, thermal energy, etc.; then the result is always the same. It's a specific number that doesn't change, unless you change the way in which the underlying quantities are measured.

Then there's the more loose usage of the word energy. When someone says "that person has a good energy," to mean that the person is generally helpful and happy, they're not using the word energy in a way that's consistent with physics. They use the word "energy" to mean well, who knows. But it's not as if they're referring to a specific numerical formula for deciding that person's "energy."

In this looser context, what is positive energy? It really depends on the person, and I doubt you'll have a definition that has any widespread consistency. It's one of those phrases that means kind of whatever the person wants it to mean, and for that reason doesn't seem very useful to me.

Positive thinking can be defined as the method to achieve health and happiness. It concentrates on positive qualities such as inner peace, strength, love, joy and happiness. In this direction research the positive psychology. Positive thinking is a mental technique that must be practiced wisely. It should not be misused to repress feelings such as sadness, depression, loneliness, etc. Optimism is a mental attitude that interprets situations and events as being best optimized. A common idiom used to illustrate optimism versus pessimism is a glass with water at the halfway point, where the optimist is said to see the glass as half full, but the pessimist sees the glass as half empty. Optimism may be linked to health. Optimists have been shown to live healthier lifestyles which may influence disease. For example, optimists smoke less, are more physically active, consume more fruit, vegetables and whole-grain bread, and consume more moderate amounts of alcohol.

The relationship between optimism and health has also been studied with regards to physical symptoms, coping strategies and negative affect for those suffering from rheumatoid arthritis, asthma, and fibromyalgia. A meta-analysis has confirmed the assumption that optimism is related to psychological well-being: "Put simply, optimists emerge from difficult circumstances with less distress than do pessimists. Optimists seem intent on facing problems head-on, taking active and constructive steps to solve their problems; pessimists are more likely to abandon their effort to attain their goals.

The psychological learning theory suggests that positive thinking can be learned. An athlete trains for several weeks or months an external behavior. He carries a certain behavior, and after some time he masters it. Thoughts can be understood as the internal behavior of a person. When we consciously practice some time a positive mental behavior, then our mind accustoms to positive thinking. It automatically responds to certain external situations with positive thoughts.

Positive thoughts lead to positive feelings. And positive feelings lead to health and happiness. To train positive thoughts has a great gain. It gives us a happy and healthy life. Especially if we practice also regularly sports yoga, walking, enough relaxation enough breaks, enough sleep, daily meditating and a healthy diet at least an apple a day.

The learning method consists of four steps. First, we need a positive thought system that suits us like the philosophy of happiness. The philosophy of happiness teaches to make the happiness to the center of life. The essence of the philosophy of happiness is the five qualities of wisdom, peace, love, strength and joy. These five properties we practice every day.

The second step is systematically to train positive thoughts. The best way is to remember every morning on the five positive qualities. We create a positive plan of the day. We get up with a positive thought. We retain our positive vision during the day. And at night we think about the day and what we can do better the next day. We feel our negative emotions fear, anger, grief, addiction. There are Helpful positive phrases are, "I'm a winner. I reach my goals. Wisdom is to organize my life so that I can live healthy and happy".

The third step is to observe consistently our thoughts throughout the day, and to stop all negative thoughts. If we recognize a negative thought, we push him away immediately. We consider what positive thought is helpful right now. We develop a positive thought and set it in place of the negative thought. If we make this at the long term, our negative thoughts are becoming less and our positive thoughts grow more and more. Nils was able to overcome his depression by this technique.

The constant observation of thought is the essence of positive thinking. Often we overcome our negative thoughts already through the constant observation of our mind. We are aware of our negative thoughts and that already deprives them their power. Sometimes we have to intervene forcefully. And just at the beginning of our mental work we should be relatively strict with our thoughts. If our inner children are educated well, we can give them a little more freedom.

The fourth step is the stabilization of positive thinking. It is not easy all day to control our negative thoughts. We need strong helpers to keep us on our long-term path of inner happiness. Such helpers are the daily spiritual reading in a book, the daily oracle reading, the daily meditation, walking and a group of positive thinking people. Very good it is to distribute some caregivers throughout the day. We create our system of daily happiness exercises. We're putting so many exercises for us in right intervals in the day that we keep ourselves constantly on the path of the positive. We stay with perseverance on our way of wisdom and happiness. If we fall off the path once, we stand up again next day. In particularly difficult situations helps the constant change of lying hearing meditation music, reading praying, chanting, sports yoga, walking and work doing well to others.

We are practicing it for so long until our negative emotions have calmed down und we are positive again. The supreme principle of conduct in suffering situations is outwardly behaving properly and at the same time managing the thoughts and feelings as well as possible. Is the difficult situation outside gone, we can heal our emotional wounds. At certain points of the problem we got inner tensions. These tensions must be resolved again when the external stress situation is over. When we don´t heal our self after stress situations, they remain permanently in our mind. In the long term they affect our mental well-being. They lead to neurotic behavior and can cause physical illnesses.

If a problem affects you emotionally, it is good to do a helpful ritual. Think first about the problem. Thinking leads to constructive engagement with the problem. You realize that you can do something. You are not a helpless victim. You can live as a winner. You can solve the problem in any way. What is your helpful idea about your problem? "My idea is".

Read a few pages in a spiritual book. Think about which book you need now. A spiritual book has a positive energy field. If we spend some time in this energy field, we get a positive spirit. Read book which will strengthen your positive energy. Read it! After reading, take a walk for an hour or dance 20 minutes as you like. Move all the rage and excitement out of your body. Think a Mantra a positive sentence and does a meditation stop your thinking five minutes. Then think about your problem. Usually you will come to rest mentally in half an hour. Half an hour then go just you like. Then you'll see things clearly. You will be able to have positive ideas. Make after the walk some yoga exercises creative hatha yoga and a long meditation in sitting meditation with the inner voice or lying down.

Hook up a nice music and remain lying down for so long, until your mind completely is at rest. Arise then again, eat something nice and think about what you need now. Give it yourself. Often it is very helpful to do something creative. We can paint, write, make music and express our feelings on our personal way. We can do something good for our fellow human beings and thus bring us into the energy of love.

If the problem is very big, you can do several rounds of reading, walking, doing good, enjoying and meditating. Usually you get then to the point, where peace arises within you. Be very gentle with you and heal emotionally more and more. If a problem cannot be solved in one day, stop after a while you're thinking about the problem. Forbid you every further reflection. Avoid harmful rumination, which leads to nothing and only reinforces the internal stress. For large problems, you can take every day a certain time for problem handling.

To solve emotional problems is a creative process. You must feel exactly what you need now. What is currently the best way to solve your problem, to find inner peace and positivity? People are different and require different strategies. It is important to avoid self-defeating behaviors, such as tablets, smoke, drink, drugs, alcohol or eating too many sweets. It is better to manage the problem with the techniques of inner happiness. Then we grow spiritually on our problems. We grow inwardly on the problems of life until we will find everlasting happiness.

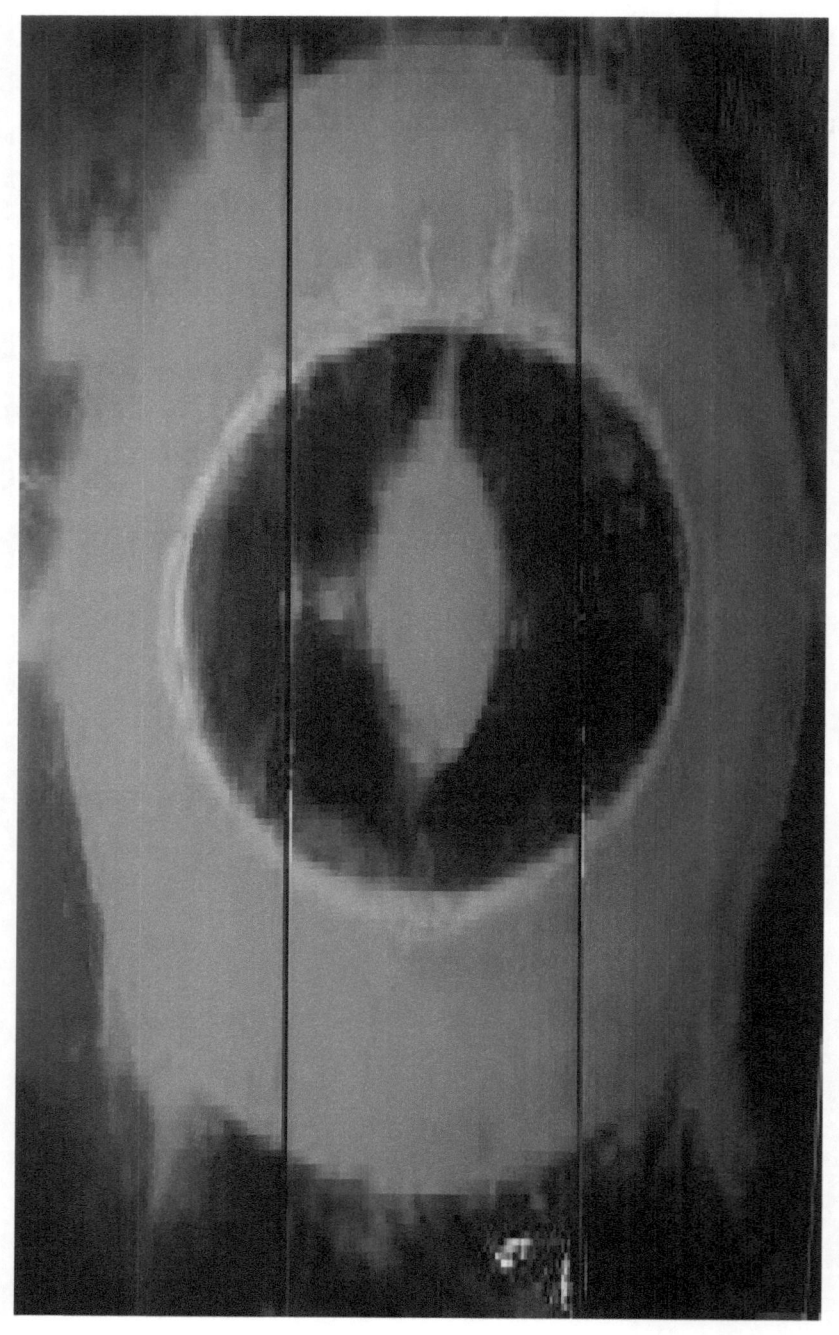

CHAPTER ONE

HOW TO BRING POSITIVE ENERGY INTO YOUR LIFE

Staying positive can be tough. Positivity can start to win when you are bombarded with a succession of negativity, failures, disappointment and heartbreak. Every challenge you face withdraws from your energy, resilience and a little bit of your faith. Once your positive energy is depleted, pessimism slowly begins to creep in and take hold.

To help you stay positive, I will tell you the secrets to revive positive energy in this article so you can try out all these ways to lead happy life.Positive thinking is a mental and emotional state of mind that focuses on the good and expects positive outcomes.

Developing and maintaining positive energy involves more than merely thinking happy thoughts. It is the anticipation of good   happiness, health, success and it is the belief that all things situations, obstacles and difficulties will work out favorably in the end.

Optimism does not involve ignoring negativity. It is the acknowledgement of the negative but then choosing to focus on the positive. At its root, it is simply the belief that despite the current circumstances things will work out favorable in the end.

20 ways to revive positive energy

If you want to stay positive when facing challenges and negative situations, here are 20 things you can do to help revive your positive energy:

- Enjoy nature

Research shows that reveling in the great outdoors promotes human health. Spending time in serene natural environments has been scientifically proven to lower stress levels, improve working memory and provide a sense of rejuvenation.

- Perform random acts of kindness

Finding ways to put a smile on the face of others affects you just as much as it affects them. It takes the focus off of you and your problems and allows you to be a positive force in the lives of others.

Doing well for others makes you feel good. It lifts your mood, improves self-esteem and self-worth and it serves as a small distraction from your current challenges.

-Develop an attitude of gratitude

Noticing and appreciating the positives in our lives is a great way to lift your spirits and provide yourself a mental boost.

-Take a mental break

Exhaustion is the silent killer of positivity. Learn to take breaks when things get overwhelming. Do something that gives your mind a break from whatever challenge you are facing–and that could just mean taking a nap.

- Laugh

Laughter truly is the best medicine for most of what ails us. Laughter strengthens your immune system, boosts mood, diminishes pain, and protects you from the damaging effects of stress.

Find a way to laugh–often. Watch a comedy; spend the evening with your crazy friend who knows how to keep you in stitches. Host a game night with your friends.

- Hang around with positive people

Research suggests that stress is contagious and the more you surround yourself with it, the more likely you are to let it affect your thoughts. In the same way that stress and negativity are contagious, so is happiness.

"You are the average of the five people you spend the most time with." The bottom line here is our behavior and thought patterns mirror those we hang around. Choose carefully who you allow into your circle.

- Look for the silver lining immediately

Trying to force optimistic thinking amidst emotional turmoil or a bit shocked usually don't work that well. Training you to look for the lesson and find the bright spot not only eases the burden a little, it also slowly begins to transform your entire thought process.

-Breathe deeply

Breathing exercises help expel toxic air from your body and refills your body and more importantly–your brain with fresh air. It clears your mind and allows you to regain mental clarity. One moment of clarity at the right time can change everything.

- Don't dwell on negativity

Avoid dwelling on downers. Downers bring you down! Focusing on negatives isn't just unpleasant; it also makes you less effective in tackling other tasks you face. Negativity produces more negativity. Bad things happen so, try not to replay them over and over and fixate on un-pleasantries. Play positive scenes in your mind instead.

-Engage in positive self-talk

Talk to yourself. Tell yourself things are going to turn around and will work out in the end. Say it out loud. Speaking what you believe out loud reinforces and strengthens the message. You say it and hear it simultaneously.

Here is a step-by-step guide to help you engage in positive self-talk: How to Stop Negative Self-Talk from Ruining Your Life

- Talk it out with a friend

Find a positive friend (or small group of friends) or confidant to talk to. Talking helps you hear the problem, admit and discuss your feelings and it gives you another set of eyes and ears working on the problem. You may find that brainstorming with another person or even a group will help you come up with new ideas to help you resolve the issue. It also reassures you that someone has your back and that emotional support makes a difference. Think of it as a low-budget therapy.

-Take a walk

Scientists have found that one of the best ways to chase the blues away is by going for a walk. A brisk Walk or calms you down by sparking nerve cells in the brain that relax the senses.

- Engage in rigorous exercise

Getting sweaty is not just good for your heart–it's good for your head too! Research on anxiety, depression and exercise shows that the psychological and physical benefits of exercise help reduce anxiety and elevate your mood. When you engage in vigorous physical activity, the "feel good" brain chemicals (neurotransmitters, endorphins and end cannabinoids) are released that ease feelings of negativity. It distracts you from your issues, and it physically relaxes you.

Find yourself too busy to do exercises? Here are 5 Ways to Find Time for Exercise

-Sleep

Proper rest is a critical part of maintaining a positive attitude. Studies have shown that even partial sleep deprivation has a significant effect on your mental state. Researchers from University of Pennsylvania discovered that subjects who were limited to less than 5 hours of sleep a night for one week felt significantly more stressed, angry, sad, and mentally exhausted.

- Journal

Journaling is a great way to deal with overwhelming emotions. It provides a healthy outlet in which you can express yourself and manage your emotions and overall mental health.

Keeping a journal can help you identify and track the causes of negative thinking and develop a mitigation plan.

-Play hooky

Taking the occasional break from the daily grind is fun, freeing and necessary. Figure out what makes you feel alive and happy and do that. Whether it's watching Netflix in your all day or if it's kayaking down a river–the goal is to have fun–whatever that means to you.

- Treat yourself

Rewarding yourself with "I time" and celebrating who you are as a person is vital to sustaining a positive outlook. Find small, meaningful and healthy ways to indulge yourself from time to time.

-Move through your day mindfully

Worry and dwelling on pervasively stressful thoughts with are optimism assassins. Living mindfully involves consciously deciding to be fully present in each moment. When you throw all of your attention, energy and resources on the now, you don't have the space for negative thoughts or worrying.

- Take care of yourself spiritually

Paying attention to and investing in you spiritually is something most people neglect. You watch what you eat, workout, try to get enough sleep and do all the things you should to keep your body and mind fit and functioning. But part of maintaining good mental health and a positive state of mind is soul care.

Take time to feed your soul and keep the mind- body-spirit connection strong by engaging in spirit enhancing, contemplative activities such as meditation, prayer, reading spiritual materials and/or attending religious services.

-Celebrate small wins

Who doesn't love a good celebration? Celebrating small victories is one of the quickest ways to give negativity the boot. Getting out of bed this morning is a win! Celebrate it. If you stayed in bed today and got a little extra rest–that too is a win! Instead of focusing on pending doom or sulking over losses–actively seek out and celebrate the things you do well and a things you did get right today.

CHAPTER TWO

TRANSFORM ANXIETY INTO POSITIVE ENERGY

Worry/anxiety is a vibrational match to humiliation, dread, and unhappiness, all of which I do not want to feel. Therefore, if I worry about the possibility of encountering other situations that are going to bring me other emotions that I don't want to experience, I will actually be setting myself to experience them!

The reason why I want things to work out in my favor is that I want to feel a certain way. Having enough money for my next endeavor, a trustworthy vehicle, and environmental happiness make me feel safe, secure, confident, grounded, happy, and at ease.

To open up to these feelings, I need to match that vibration emotionally—and non-stop worrying does not match. If I want self-confidence, happiness, and security, I have to skip ahead to feeling that way now. If you find yourself fraught with anxiety, feeling fearful about the future, you will attract your worst fears. When anxiety tries to bring us down, there are 3 things we can do:

- Take a moment and see what feelings underlie your fears.

Then see if you can figure out how you'd rather feel and choose to feel that feeling instead. If you are having a hard time lifting your mood, get busy doing something you enjoy that will raise your positive vibration.

It's easy to raise our vibration. Engaging in our hobbies is a great way to bump our vibes up a few notches, and it can be anything really—playing sports, cooking, baking, gardening, playing music, cleaning, exercising, meditating, practicing yoga, singing, dancing, crafting, building, organizing, or snuggling with your pet. When we keep ourselves elevated, it's really hard for anxiety to find us, helping to keep negative experiences at bay.

- Instead of gripping at fear and worrying about whether or not something will work out, just know that it will.

This is what it means to have faith. Just know that no matter what the outcome, you will be okay, and if it is in your highest interest to have what you want, you will have it.

- And last, ask the universe for what you want and then let go of the outcome.

Instead of focusing on what you want, focus on how you can be of service. When we are serving others, we are tapping into more of that feel-good energy, which will bring us more feel-good experiences.

Show up each day ready to serve the world, your family, your environment, and yourself. Focus on how you can add value to the lives of others. Good experiences will come to you. Once we realize the root of anxiety, it is easier for us to transform it into positivity. I wish you all a blissful day!

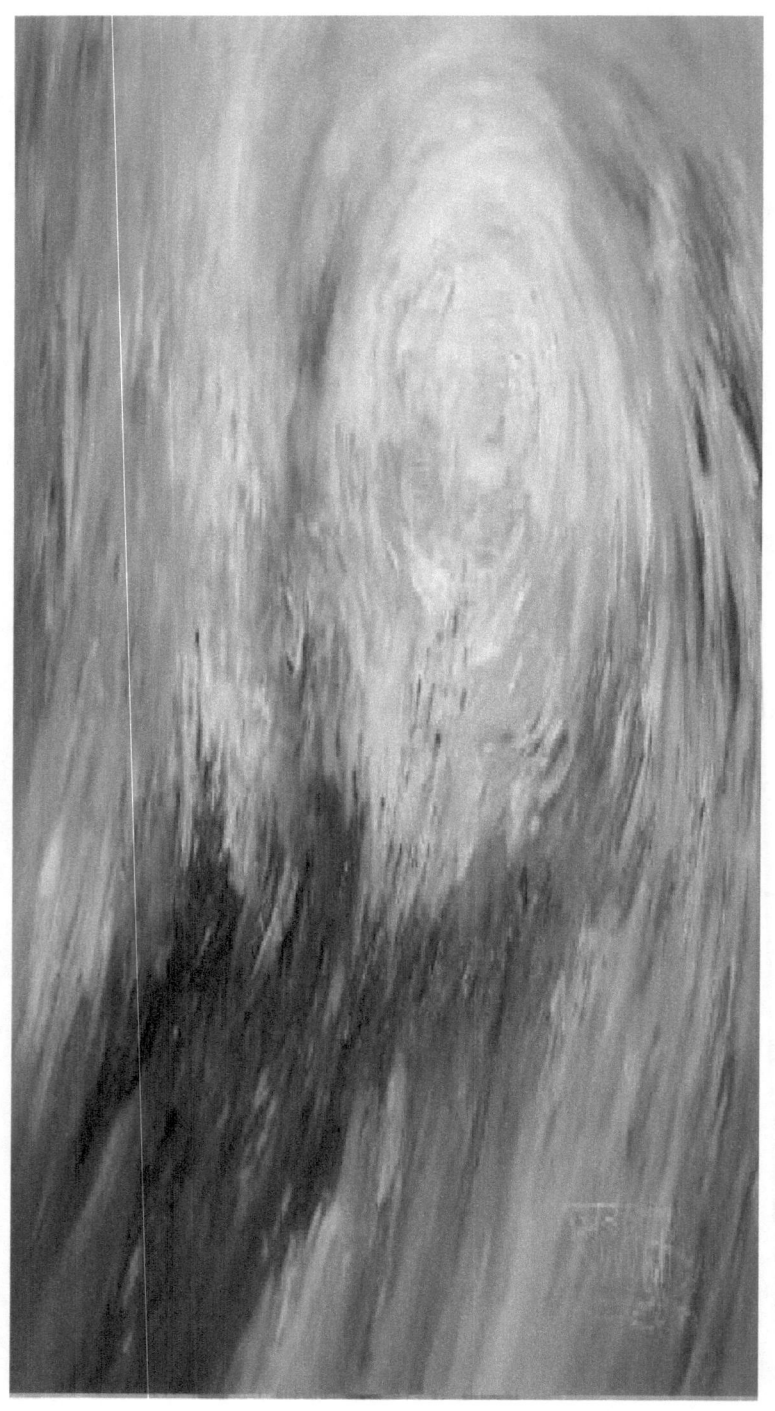

CHAPTER THREE

HOW TO USE POSITIVE ENERGY TO SUCCEED

Right now there's an energy field or aura around you that others can feel. Without saying anything you can emit a sense of peace, calm and other positive feelings that can inspire, uplift and energize the people with whom you come in contact.

On the other hand, you can repel people by giving off negative vibes such as tension, anxiety and anger. People who do so are called energy vampires, says Dr. Judith Oroff, psychiatrist and author of a slew of books, including Positive Energy: Extraordinary Prescriptions for Transforming Fatigue, Stress and Fear into Vibrancy, Strength and Love. "These are people who can suck you dry and make you tired and depressed and worn out and feel like you want to nap," she says.

By all means does not be that person. If you want to succeed in business and life, you should aim to be magnetic, likeable and someone others want to be around. In other words, you want to emit positive energy. Here's Orloff's advice on how to do it.

-Change your thoughts.

If you're thinking negative thoughts, just stop. Intentionally focus on the positive things happening in your life. "Let's say you're turning into a victim. Like 'Poor me. Everybody's against me. Nobody at work appreciates me. I'm never going to get my raise.' You're working yourself up in a negative frenzy," she says. 'You have to stop yourself and [think] 'No, I'm not going there.'" Think of it this way: Modern conveniences alone have elevated your quality of life immeasurably compared with the billions of people who have lived and died on this planet over the course of history. You have countless things for which to be grateful.

-Improve your mood.

Listen to good music. Seek out a good laugh. Have sex when you get the opportunity. Or, engage in what Orloff calls a "three-minute positive energy meditation." It involves shutting the door to distractions, relaxing and focusing on a beautiful power image such as a sunset or waterfall. "You just take three minutes to shift and visualize something very positive," she says.

-Take care of your body.

Exercise, for one thing. It gets endorphins--which act like morphine in the body--flowing to trigger positive feelings. Eat fruits, vegetables and other healthy foods. Avoid sugar and diet soda. Limit alcohol and caffeine consumption.

-Treat others well.

Don't gossip. Look at how you can serve others, help your coworkers and add something positive to your environment. Or off also suggests "surrendering comparisons," which involves ceasing to want what other people have. "Rather, focus on what you do have and if you admire somebody then learn from them," she says. "Envy and jealousy...create negative energy."

CHAPTER FOUR

MOTIVATIONAL QUOTES ABOUT SUCCESS AND LIFE WHICH GIVE YOU POSITIVE ENERGY

Inspirational quotes and motivational sayings have an amazing ability to change the way we feel about life. This is why I find them so interesting and crucial on our paths to success. So what's their secret?

You see, the way you think and feel about yourself, including your beliefs and expectations about what is possible for you, determines everything that happens to you.

When you change the quality of your thinking, you change the quality of your life, sometimes instantly. Just as positive words can make someone smile or a well-timed humorous quote can make someone laugh, our thoughts react to the world in real-time.

You have complete control over only one thing in the universe your thinking – and that's where motivational quotes come in !Jump to the quotes you're looking for now: Inspirational Quotes about Life, Quotes for Students, and Motivational Quotes for Work, Success Quotes or Leadership Quotes.

You can decide what you are going to think in any given situation. Your thoughts and feelings determine your actions and determine the results you get. It all starts with your thoughts – and I have found that inspirational words are a quick way to retune your thinking.

Try keeping a few uplifting excerpts or positive proclamations on hand. If you ever notice your energy or your spirit begin to drop, simply recite an inspirational and uplifting quote to quickly boost your mood.

I've compiled a list of some of the best motivational quotes so you can start the year by taking control of your thoughts, thinking positively and setting new goals.

1- The Way Get Started Is To Quit Talking And Begin Doing.

This straight-to-business quote comes from the man who created the happiest place on earth – and a multibillion-dollar empire.

2- The Pessimist Sees Difficulty In Every Opportunity. The Optimist Sees Opportunity in Every Difficulty

When it comes to success quotes by famous people, Winston Churchill's inspirational words of wisdom always make the list.

3-Don't Let Yesterday Take Up Too Much Of Today.

Will Rogers was an American actor, cowboy, columnist and social commentator who believed in keeping forward momentum. .

4- You Learn More From Failure Than From Success. Don't Let It Stop You.

When you replace 'lose' with 'learn' in your vocabulary, the thought of failure becomes less daunting and lets you focus on growth.

5- It is not whether you get knocked down; it's Whether You Get Up.

Vince Lombardi was an American football hero whose uplifting words frequently make it onto Top 10 Inspirational Quotes lists.

6- If You Are Working On Something That You Really Care About, You Don't Have To Be Pushed. The Vision Pulls You.

Steve Jobs truly captured some of the wisdom of life in this statement. Do that which you are passionate about and your work will feel effortless .Motivational ocean view with Steve Jobs quote about working with your passion

7-People, Who Are Crazy Enough To Think They Can Change The World, Are The Ones Who Do.

This is one of the best quotes to live by because it reminds me to think without limits and never doubt my wildest thoughts.

8- Failure Will Never Overtake Me If My Determination To Succeed Is Strong Enough.

There's a special place in my heart for these inspirational words. They remind me of my unwavering determination to become a motivational speaker.

9-Entrepreneurs Are Great At Dealing With Uncertainty And Also Very Good At Minimizing Risk. That's The Classic Entrepreneur.

This line always puts a smile on my face because it alludes to the excitement of not knowing what to expect but seeing a possible life-changing outcome.

10- We May Encounter Many Defeats But We Must Not Be Defeated.

Maya Angelou was one of the top civil rights activists and embraced a spirit of positive thinking and sheer determination. maya-angelou-we-may-encounter-defeats-but-we-must-not-be-defeated.

Use them to stay motivated as you learn how to write a book, become a better speaker, or set and achieve every SMART Goal on your path to success. They hold within them one of the greatest keys to success: positive energy!

CHAPTER FIFE

HOW DOES POSITIVE ENERGY ATTRACT

POSITIVE ENERGY?

Every moment you have a choice – to be at peace or to be in resistance. When you are at peace, you attract positive energy and when you resist you create negative vibes that reflect back on your being. It's a simple choice that you need to make.

It's not your boss, colleagues, parents, ex or the traffic, but your own perception that creates stress and negative energy. Circumstances are neutral. You will generate positive vibes when your inner state is one of alignment and congruence, instead of being in resistance.

Here are a few tips to attract positive energy into your life by staying in touch with your inner peace and stillness.

-Listen to Uplifting Music

The right music can heal and raise our vibrations. Create a playlist of songs that have a positive effect on you. Listen to this playlist every morning immediately after waking up or while getting ready for the day. Dance or move your body to the rhythm if you feel like. This is a great way to get your share of exercise for the day and in doing so, shake off that lethargic/draining energy from your body. If you don't feel like dancing, do some shaking Qigong.

- Treat Everyone the Way You Want to be treated.

A day is easily ruined when you start holding resentment against someone. Know that everything is oneness and though we appear as different forms, everything is the manifestation of the one true essence. When you see others as yourself you will not harbor negative feelings and in turn your attitude will attract positive energy from the people around you.

- Let Go of Your Need to Control

Life is a flux and its nature is change. The more you resist the more a particular situation will persist. Whenever you try to control a life situation, you will feel stressed out and this will generate a lot of negative energy.

Just imagine life to be a raging river, does it serve any purpose to struggle? Wouldn't it be much more relaxing and peaceful if you just let go and allow yourself to float with the flow? People who stay surrendered and relaxed generate a lot of positive energy and attract the grace of life.

- Learn to See the Positive in Every Situation

Know that good and bad are just perceptions created in the conditioned mind. In reality every life situation is pure grace and is the manifestation of the one truth – call it God or Spirit or Energy. When you see every situation with this innocence, it will reveal its grace to you.

- Visualize a Peaceful Life

Your mind might be addicted to negative thinking; most minds are. You will have to consciously break out of this addiction if you want to attract good energy within you.

Stay conscious and see your mind churning out fearful images. Now, instead of giving energy to these thoughts divert your attention to visualizing a peaceful flow of life. Envision feeling calm and fulfilled. You will be amazed at the positive vibes you feel in your body.

- Stop Worrying About the Future

Worry has not served any purpose to this date for anyone. Whatever has to happen will happen, there is nothing you will achieve by worrying about it. In fact what you worry about will not even happen most of the times. So why waste energy dwelling on worries?

You are unconsciously creating a lot of negative energy inside you which is harmful to your whole being. Just plan practically and leave the rest to life.

- Drop the Resentment Within

The past is past; it has no reality than as a memory trace. Can you live in such simplicity? After all if you don't continuously think up a bad memory you will not feel any resentment within. So just learn to forgive and move on. There is a lot positive energy in the simple act of forgiveness.

- Stay as the Presence Instead of the Ego

The present moment holds a lot of power within. You can tap into this power by learning to experience the present moment fully. As Eckhart Tolle puts it, 'Be here fully!'

Whatever task you are doing, try to become fully conscious of it. Be conscious of your surroundings, your thoughts and your actions. Of-course you cannot be present all the time, but do this exercise whenever you feel the need to relax and attract some good vibes.

- Be in Nature

A simple way to attract good energy is to be in nature. Just look at the nature around you for a while. A tree or a flower; it just rests in stillness and moves with the wind.

There is a peace that radiates from their being. This peace will ignite your own inner true nature of stillness.

You can also consider having some indoor plants. According to color psychology green is the color of balance and harmony. Which is why, having indoor plants can bring a sense of peace to your inner being.

- Make a list of all the things you want to come into your life over the next 12 months.

Light a candle and burn the list, releasing your wishes so the universe can provide them. Open your front door to allow this new energy to enter.

- MAKE A CHANGE.

Large or small revisions help to welcome in new energy. So go ahead, get a haircut, change your route to work, make a conscious effort to recycle or take ballroom dancing lessons and enjoy!

- Have Vibrant Colors around

Color therapy is getting popular by the day. Colours emit vibrations that affect our psyche. e.g.: Yellow gives confidence, Red signifies security, Orange signifies emotional balance and blue improves communication and intuition. Explore its benefits in daily life. Change your drapes, bed sheets; pillow covers etc. with primary colors or any colour that makes you happy. Light coloured candles. Wear more vibrant hues. Choose outfits depending on the way you want to protect yourself.

- Embrace the Love of a Child

Children have a natural energy that is so vibrant that it is a blessing for most adults to experience it. Speak or share experiences daily with a child in your family and you will be well on your way to seeing life in a very different way.

- Energize your house

Light a candle or diya every morning and evening. Fire has capacity to burn negative energies. Fill your house with fragrance and aromas that relax the mind. Try and have a water body. Also have open windows; the flow of air takes away negative energy.

- Inner child therapy

Each person has an inner child within him/her. Do things you used to as a child be it clay modeling, doodling, drawing with colour pencils/crayons or even jumping into a puddle. They help you get rid of inhibitions and help you explore new areas of life.

- Clear Clutter

Clear your home, work station and even your car. Most importantly, clear your mind. Clutter creates blocks in the flow of energy within you. When these blocks remain for long, it spreads all over your body and mind leaving you in a forever irritable and snappy mood.

CHAPTER SIX

WHAT IS THE DIFFERENCE BETWEEN POSITIVE AND NEGATIVE ENERGY?

As you know, it is a drastically different experience being around positive people versus negative ones. If you are striving to be more positive yourself, here are 15 ways you can do so:

- "Failure is part of learning."

Positive people view failure as an opportunity to learn and get better. They understand that failure is an event, and doesn't define who they are. Negative people are emotionally disabled by failure because they allow it to define who they are. They fail to understand that it's part of the learning and growing process.

- "I can do hard things."

Positive people love to be challenged. They understand that there is no growth without struggle. Positive people embrace difficulty, and look for ways to overcome them.

Negative people love the easy road. Because obstacles increase the likelihood of failure, they try to avoid them like the plague. To negative people, hard times don't make you, they break you.

- "I always give my best."

Positive people focus on giving their best effort, regardless of the situation. They understand that there are many things they cannot control, but effort is not one of them. No matter what, the positive person strives to give their best — even if it isn't much. Negative people want things to come easy to them. If they have to try hard, they believe they just aren't good at it and give up. They are more likely to give their absolute best if they know people are watching them.

- "She is inspiring!"

Positive people are inspired by the success of others, they look at those who are excelling and ask themselves the question, "What can I learn from them?" Negative people become jealous and threatened by the success of others. To negative people, when others succeed it means they are failing.

- "What can I do better?"

Positive people embrace feedback. Because they are always striving to get better, they are open to learn anything that will enhance their skill set. Negative people get offended when they receive correction or feedback. Instead of seeing it as means to improve, they interpret feedback as a sign of their incompetence.

- "I give power to what I focus on."

Positive people focus on things they can control. They understand that their happiness is dependent on how they choose to respond to what happens to them. Positive people believe that they give power to what they focus on, so they use it wisely. Negative people center their focus on things they can't control. For example, they ruminate over past conversations, beat themselves up on past mistakes, and allow their fear of the future to stop them in their tracks today.

- "People can change."

Positive people know that the only thing that doesn't change is *change*. They believe that they can change, and that other people can change. Negative people believe that people are fixed; therefore, they don't try to improve because they believe, "What's the use?" Additionally, negative people don't allow others to change. Once a negative person puts a label on something, it's very difficult for them to see it in a different way.

- "I still have a lot to learn."

Positive people love to learn. They understand information evolves, and what used to work 10-years ago, might not be effective today. Negative people believe they know it all, and are less likely to welcome new information if it contradicts what they believe. They care less about what's right, and more about who's right.

- "Let's go big!"

A positive person isn't afraid to swing for the fences because they don't fear striking out. A negative person not only thinks small, but they also try to convince others that their dreams and aspirations are too big.

- "Have you heard about [insert name]?"

Positive people build others up when they aren't around. Negative people tear people down to make themselves feel good.

- "I am my own worst enemy or best friend."

Positive people have effective self-talk. They are aware of the story they tell themselves, and don't allow their own thoughts to discourage them. Additionally, they are realistic with their expectations. Positive people don't feed themselves lies about their weaknesses or how difficult the situation is. Instead, they tell themselves what they need to do to succeed. Negative people are their own worst enemy. They struggle to see the bright side of anything, even if they are successful. They are also masterful at focusing on all the negative aspects, and diminishing their own confidence.

- "What is my body saying?"

Positive people carry themselves like champions. They are purposeful in the way they interact with people and their facial expressions show positivity. Negative people carry themselves small. They hang their heads, and look down. Just by looking at them, you would think they are mad, sad, or indifferent definitely not happy.

- "Teamwork makes the dream work."

Because they are team players, positive people will get behind and support ideas that are not theirs — even if they might disagree with it. Negative people have a hard time fully supporting ideas they feel won't be successful. When an idea that wasn't theirs doesn't succeed, they are sure to give their teammates the "I-told-you-so" expression.

- "What's the bright side?"

Positive people have an attitude of gratitude. They can see the good in a situation, and don't take things for granted. Negative people struggle to see the silver-lining in difficult situations. They don't often take the time to stop and notice the positive aspects of a situation.

-"You're so good!"

Positive people like to spread positivity. They pay close attention to when others do well, and they are quick to tell them. Negative people say, "Why would I compliment people for things they are supposed to do?" What they don't understand is, it's not about the compliment, and it's about showing the other person that you notice them. A simple compliment can strengthen relationships and motivate the person to do even better. Positive people don't underestimate the power of encouraging words.

CHAPTER SEVEN

POSITIVE ENERGY AND THE EDUCATION

To make education systems work optimally towards the learning goals and to do so for every single student in the system, we need to understand how learning works. We need to fully grasp what it is that turns students' energy into the development we envisage. Although much remains to be uncovered, there is much about learning processes that we have discovered over the past few decades.

For one, learning is about connecting. To learn, people need to be able to connect the new with what is already known. To a great extent, prior knowledge determines what can be learnt; the learning outcome of human activity heavily depends on the extent to which new information can be connected with what has already been acquired. Research into learning has tended to highlight the cognitive side of this basic insight. However, especially in compulsory education systems enlisting children and adolescents, the cognitive aspects of learning (and connecting) cannot be separated from other dimensions of learning. For young learners of flesh and blood, the cognitive aspects of learning are inextricably entwined with social, emotional and physical aspects.

Connections, then, may be hypothesized to be richer for learning and thus give rise to more sustainable energy-learning cycles, if they positively engage the learner's whole being. Therefore, in this line of reasoning, learning is facilitated if learners also connect socio-emotionally to what they aim to learn or need to learn and if learners socio-emotionally connect to the activity they are participating in and might learn from. In addition, learning will be enhanced if learners are able or willing to connect to the person(s) with whom they are interacting and/or from whom they are learning.

In other words, the combination of socio-emotional, physical and cognitive engagement can top-up the energy unleashed for learning, and the learning experience, in turn, may feed the learner's socio-emotional, physical and cognitive well-being. Secondly, learning is an active verb. Connecting (and thus learning) cannot be done for the learner; it is something the learner needs to do. For much of what people need to learn, especially for the development of complex competences, people need to engage in situated practice and to do so repeatedly. However, merely repeating a particular activity does not automatically result in deep-level learning. Much learning requires some degree of reflection on what we are doing.

If we understand what we are doing (especially when we are doing, or supposed to be doing, new and complex things), our capacity to handle the new, modify and apply it in a wide range of situations and contexts may be largely enhanced. In this way, learners' natural powers to learn will turn into expert power. The above implies that much learning requires effort and that learning also has a motivational aspect. If learners assign personal meaning to what is to be learnt or done, if they believe the new will make a positive difference in their lives, if they expect the learning or participating will matter in any way, if they can make educational aims their aims, they might be inclined to invest more energy in the activity.

Ultimately, much of what does engage people in activities that might lead to learning boils down to some prospect of personal or social reward. In sum, learning is about connecting, investing, and expecting. The three reinforce each other. If people can connect the new they encounter in the now to something they knew, did or felt in the past with a view to feeling or doing better in the future, then they are bound to invest energy in the ongoing activity, and the energy-learning wheel will start turning. This does not imply that learners need to be consciously aware of each of these conditions. There is quite a lot of investing, connecting and expecting that goes on at an unconscious level.

Conversely, the socially-disadvantaged child who cannot connect her prior knowledge and skills that she developed at home to the abstract subject-matter of the school curriculum, who feels that the teacher holds low expectations of her school achievement and who expects to do badly on the following tests, may find it increasingly hard to invest further mental and physical energy into studying and working hard at school. For this student, the energy-learning cycle may grind to a halt: the energy for learning this student has left may fail to be renewed.

Designing Learning-Oriented Education systems work well if they work well for every single student in the system. That is, if they manage to keeps the self-perpetuating energy-learning cycle of every single child going and if they make sure that every single child develops the crucial competences in the curriculum and realizes her full learning potential.

They challenge and trust learners: Teachers in successful education systems hold high expectations of every single student in the system and expose their students to challenging, meaningful content.

Challenge is key to high-quality education, because, in essence, it is about inviting learners to stretch their muscles and continuously acquire new skills, knowledge and attitudes. Reviewing the research on what distinguishes expert teachers (whose students show higher-than-average learning gains year after year) and experienced teachers, Hattie concludes that "expert teachers do differ from experienced teachers, particularly in the degree of challenge that they present to students, and, most critically, in the depth to which students learn to process information." They activate and motivate learners: teachers cannot do the learning for their learners.

Research into learning processes amply shows that to develop expertise (in whichever field), learners need to engage in much deliberate practice, during which they can learn by doing and by reflecting on what they are doing in an effort to improve their practice . Rephrasing this insight in terms of sustainable education, this means that learners need to invest energy in their own learning process. As research into learning motivation indicates, energy for learning is boosted and activated if learners are exposed to tasks they consider valuable, challenging and doable and if they know that support (by a more competent partner) is provided should obstacles arise.

In addition, learners' energy for engaging in learning activities might further be boosted to the extent that teachers tailor content and support to their students' learning needs and allow their students to have a say in what learning content and learning activities are truly worthwhile.

Therefore, in successful education systems, the substantial body of decontextualized knowledge students need to acquire is linked by teachers to numerous concrete, contextualized cases and examples and connected to students' prior experience; in a similar vein, students are invited to apply this knowledge to new cases in (semi-) authentic contexts and situations.

Both inside and outside school, learners should be offered rich opportunities to re-contextualize their new knowledge to fully understand it, to make it come alive, to put it to societal use and to use it to enrich their own and other people's lives. Therefore, in sustainable education, bridges between the school and the outside world are constructed and maintained: opportunities for workplace learning, community learning and learning from the multimodal experiences that modern technology offers are fully exploited to allow the learners to establish rich connections between the abstract and the concrete, between academic knowledge and real life and between new knowledge and learners' prior knowledge.

CHAPTER EIGHT

HOW TO BRING MORE POSITIVE ENERGY INTO YOUR HOME

Your home can drastically affect your mood. When we're seeing, hearing, feeling, smelling, and tasting things that we like, we feed well. When we're surrounded by things that are aesthetically displeasing or trigger painful memories, we feel bad. So, it's possible to bring more positivity into your life simply by rearranging your living space.

"The energy of organized things (clothes, furniture, rooms) is bright and light," Milana Perepyolkina, author of Gypsy Energy Secrets: Turning a Bad Day into a Good Day No Matter What Life Throws at You, tells Bustle. "The energy of clutter is dark and heavy. But you don't have to be consciously aware of this energy. Most people pick up on this energy subconsciously. For thousands of years, people knew that clutter was connected to sickness. This is how we learned to be drawn to organized things: order was connected to health".

Whether you're looking to bring more positivity into your life or just boost your mood through your surroundings, a few small changes to your room or apartment can go a long way. Here are some ways to update your living space that will help you usher out old, negative energy and invite positive energy in.

-Decorate With Your Favorite Color

"Color is a powerful influencer, and the way we feel when we see a color we dislike can affect us physically," Moll Anderson, author of Change Your Home, Change Your Life with Color, tells Bustle. "We may suddenly feel exhausted, anxious, or angry, and although we may not understand why, it's definitely a strong aversion. You may have known you hated a color, but didn't realize the color was actually adding to your anxiety

-Make Your Bed

Your parents may have annoyed you when they told you to do this, but a made bed really can help you feel ready to start your day and go to sleep at night. "An organized environment sets the tone for the day," wellness coach Maureen Lake tells Bustle. "Try it — you'll be amazed at its power, especially when you walk into the bedroom at the end of the day, and it looks inviting and comfy. You can't wait to jump into bed at night and get a good night's sleep"!

-Clean With Intention

There's a reason people make such a big deal out of spring cleaning: Clearing old stuff out of your home can also clear out old energy. To give your cleaning extra meaning, Perepyolkina recommends the following process: "Start by cleaning your entire house; pay attention to every inch of space including walls, ceilings, carpet, doors, and windows. As you clean the walls, stroke them with love.

Spread sea salt around the bedroom and leave it for the next 24 hours to absorb the negative energy, and then vacuum it all away singing joyful songs.

Open all windows and go around the house clapping your hands, moving the negative energy out of the windows and inviting positive energy in through the doors. After the house is clean, it is time to fill it with beautiful music, songs, laughter, lovely things, and an abundance of soft fabrics".

-Fill Your Bedroom with Things That Make You Feel Safe

Our bedrooms are where we do the most vulnerable things, says Perepyolkina: sleep and sex. Therefore, it's important to feel as safe and secure as possible in them. "The fewer possessions you have in your bedroom, the better," she says. "Don't store anything under your bed; make sure your closet has only the most valuable clothes that you cherish and wear often; keep only one or two items on top of the night stands. ... Filling your bedroom with the items that you love the most insures that you get an additional protection from negative energy. Think soft and subtle fabrics (nothing bright or dark), eliminate all sharp corners, and remove plants. Talk to your pillow before you go to sleep — trust me on this — your possessions absorb good energy and then share it with you while you sleep".

-Use Bright Colors

There's a reason we sometimes use the word "bright" to mean "happy" — bright colors really do increase our happiness. "Brightening up your living space can have a remarkable effect on the energy and zen of you and your home," Caleb Backe, health and wellness expert for Maple Holistics, tells Bustle. "Brighter homes with more exposure to natural light are linked to a more positive state of mental health, whereas dim or ill-lit homes are generally found to be linked to depression and low-energy. Add more lamps, open up the shades, and purchase brighter, more powerful bulbs in order to transform and enhance the positive energy in your living space".

-Adopt a Pet or Plants

There's nothing to lift your mood like caring for another creature, even if it's just a plant. "There is a reason that house plants are the most popular housewarming gift," says Backe. "Introducing fresh, green life, flowers, a fish tank, or an herb garden gives the home a more energetic and organic feel. Replace dull decorations with living, practical decorations and feel the positive energy flow"!

-Make a Vision Board

A vision board is a collage of images and words that depict how you envision your future. This gives you "a visual reminder of the things you want to manifest in your life so that you can learn to be present and allow more positivity," Chandelle Henry, author of Muted Nation: The Skeptics Quick Guide to Tackling Depression, Anxiety and Other Soul-Sucking Ailments in a Distracting World, tells

Bustle. All you need are some magazines, scissors, glue, and a vision.

-Leave Affirmation Post-Its Around

Another way to motivate you to stay positive is to leave post-its around with inspirational quotes or affirmations. "Having reminders around the house helps to erase old narratives and welcome new ones that subconsciously stick because you keep seeing it," says Henry. Make these changes to feel more positive in your home, and you'll carry that positivity with you wherever you go.

I don't know about you, but when I look around my house and consider the various items that need to be fixed, it often feels like no money, more problems — especially when payday is a ways off. When I'm feeling that vibe, I call on the genies of the internet to help, because there's no shortage of killer Amazon products that will cut your problems in half, no matter what kind of issue you're having.

Let me just give you one example: You haven't lived until you've tried out the miracle silicone adhesive Sugru. It's just the coolest stuff, because it stays flexible while you're working with it to do everything from fix up floppy shoe soles to mount your artwork to the wall... then overnight, it hardens into a solid, complete with an air-tight, waterproof seal. My favorite use of this amazing substance is to patch my phone charger cords, since I seem to go through a cord every other day. Since the silicone doesn't conduct a current and itself serves as an insulator, it's the perfect answer to make my cords good as new, without worrying and without ordering another gross of them.

If you carry more keys than a janitor, this organizer will keep them straight while also preventing the sharp edges from making a hole in your pocket or scratching up your phone. The Italian leather sheath is equipped with a rotating bolt (it comes with three of various widths) that lock to keep your keys folded down when you're not using them. Then, simply rotate the key you wish to use around to the outside of the fob and you're ready to go.

-Clear the air.

Open your windows and let the circulation flow. If you live in a polluted area, grab an air purifier or plug in a glowing Himalayan salt lamp to get the air around you buzzing with happiness. The air is infused with negative ions after a rainstorm, so it feels extra fresh. Salt lamps send these negative ions into the air, creating a positive space.

-Deep clean.

Chances are that if you're feeling heavy or stuck, it shows in the nooks and crannies of your home. Where there's dirt and dust, there's stagnation. Stagnation is what happens when energy flow gets blocked. Acupuncture eliminates stagnation within your body, restoring optimal flow and balance. Cleaning does the same for your home.

-Add color.

Every color brings a different energy to a space. Yellows usually add radiance, greens spur growth and flexibility, reds welcome prosperity, and oranges bring warmth and cheer. While there are so many meanings to color, the best color therapists I've met have all said the same thing: Start with your favorite colors and keep them on display.

-Banish bad memories.

Photos associated with painful times, outfits from parts of your life you don't want to dwell on, furniture that you have no use for gifted from friends and family … all of it can be donated if it's not serving you. Marie Kondo's groundbreaking book, The Life-Changing Art Of Tidying Up, suggests you shouldn't live with anything that doesn't spark joy when touched. I love this philosophy — the practice can help you pare down your belongings to only the things that you absolutely love!

-Put up some art

.If a piece of art moves your spirit, it should go on a wall. Feng shui is all about feeling connected to your space, so anything visual that resonates with you is a perfect addition.

- Pamper pets.

When your animal family is happy, your home springs to life. Long walks in nature, new toys, and fresh-baked treats all of these make a pet's life extra-radiant!

-Add soft materials.

The modern world has enough hard edges. Studies show that touching soft objects increases our sense of comfort and security. Don't be afraid to add a blanket here and there or soft pillows and shag carpeting underfoot — it'll refresh your home and add more bliss to your routine.

-Turn on music.

So simple, yet very few people I know play music in the background of their home during a typical day. Music has therapeutic qualities and has been shown to increase self-esteem and foster healthy relationships.

-Get creative.

Make things. An art practice will help you to heal and balance and spark change in your life. It doesn't have to be a "serious" or "significant" hobby. Doodling, finger-painting, or getting into your favorite childhood crafts totally counts.

CHAPTER NINE

WHY IS POSITIVE ENERGY IMPORTANT IN
THE WORKPLACE?

Everything is energy. Energy is powerful enough to create your success or promote your demise. Everything you involve yourself in is a result of the energy you contribute. How you contribute to your professional environment is as important as what you contribute. You may have the experience, knowledge, skill, and a long history of success; however, if you approach a new project, a meeting, a new job, an employee, your boss, or a customer with infected/negative energy, you should also be prepared to take responsibility for the consequences.

Some experts will claim energy is neither positive nor negative, rather all energy was neutral and only has the ability to take on the form in which you give it. This couldn't be further from the truth. The reality is you do have the power to choose how you exert your own energy, but you do not always have the ability to prevent encountering others' negative energy. Sometimes it is easy to see how others affect you, but many times you may not even realize the effect others are having on you. Creating an awareness of how situations or people make you feel can help correct or deflect this negative energy.

As a leader, your energy can determine the success of a meeting, a workday or even your overall company. If you have an employee or co-worker who is struggling, have you considered how much responsibility you have in their performance?

If you have chosen the privilege and responsibility to supervise others, how are you dealing with your negative employees? Negativity is contagious. It may seem as if dealing with negative people is easier to simply ignore them. However, it's important to remember that many people are not aware of how negative energy is affecting them. Therefore, your negative employees may be consciously or sub-consciously expanding their negativity and influencing the behavior of others.

I don't mean to toot my own horn, but I thrive on creating positive energy in the workplace. And, I think I'm pretty great at it! I have been in many job reviews where that is one of the key attributes that I bring to a team. I'm proud of that. I truly believe that if you want to succeed in life, both personally and professionally, you must be "magnetic". Be that person that others want to be around. Naturally, you will see how this impacts your life...both at home, and in the workplace.

Let's start by discussing how I define energy. Some people may not realize this, but everyone has an aura, or energy field, that walks alongside us no matter what we're doing. This energy can either draw others in or it can repel them, without even having to say a word. Powerful, right? Think about it this way: When you walk down a sidewalk, is your head held high, eager to greet those who pass you with a warm smile or a "Hello"? Or do you look down at your feet or pretend to be on your phone when passing someone? These are things to think about when evaluating the kind of energy you naturally demonstrate to others.

Every day we exude good or bad energies from ourselves. This energy that we create can significantly influence our own outlook on situations, as well as everyone else's around us. So, if we make a conscious effort to create more positive energy directly from ourselves, can you imagine the improvements that could be made in our lives? Our families? Our workplace? Our communities?

Staying positive at work on a daily basis is imperative to our mental health. This is especially true since we basically spend more time with our coworkers than our own families. If we are miserable all day, it will show, and it can, in turn, cause those around us to be miserable. Who wants that? I'm a strong believer in the fact that genuine positive energy is contagious. But, at the same time, so is negativity. So, choose wisely.

- Start with Yourself. Yes, it should be that simple. Make a conscious effort to focus on gratitude, genuine integrity, and positive thoughts. Keep the typical "glass half-full" mindset on everything you do and say. Show selflessness and give off compassionate energy. Be attentive to your surroundings and other people's feelings and needs, and then offer a helping hand when it's appropriate. Nothing says positive energy more than that. And remember, it's contagious. Win-win for everyone.

- Collaboration. You know the saying, "There am No I in Team." Well, your positive or negative energy can come across very easily based on your team dynamic. Show others that their opinions and suggestions matter. Make it easy for people to come to you for your opinions and suggestions, too! Keep an "open door" approach to encourage collaboration and openness to others.

- Community Involvement

Nothing gives off positive energy more than doing something that makes you feel good. What better way to feel good and build positive energy than getting involved in your community? Staying actively involved in something you're authentically passionate about will naturally bring you feelings of accomplishment and satisfaction. These feelings will then radiate from you in the form of positive energy! Participating in a volunteer effort with your coworkers is a fantastic way to build open lines of communication through trust, participation, teamwork and most of all, fun! And again, win-win for everyone.

-Lifestyle – So many things in our daily lives can positively or negatively impact our mindset. The best way to maintain a constant, consistent flow of positive thinking is to make a conscious effort to make positive lifestyle choices.

We all know what can influence us negatively. So, don't associate with those things. Whether it's a person or a habit: let it go. Instead, focus on what brings POSITIVE energy into your life. Listen to uplifting, inspiring music. Go for a walk during your lunch break. Do yoga or meditate in the morning before work. Read more books. Keep a bowl of chocolates by your desk to encourage others to come over for a quick chat during the workday. Give praises and compliments daily. Get a dog. Or just go to the dog park and watch other people's dogs (yes, I've been known to do that!) Moral of the story: find things that make you happy and do them.

According to Positive Psychology Program, our genes are responsible for about 50% of our happiness and our actions and attitudes account for 40%. So sure, we can't argue that genuine happiness will come more naturally to some than others. But why not focus on that remaining 40% and make the most of it? You decide.

I believe we can all use our positive energy to truly succeed in life. We can have better relationships with our friends and families. In the workplace, we can use positive energy to make connections through networking, gain new clients, be more productive and efficient which can lead to promotions, and of course, make new friends in the process!

CHAPTER TEN

HOW TO FEED YOUR MIND WITH POSITIVE
ENERGY TO HAVE A GREAT LIFE

Most of us don't know this, and even if we know, we don't believe in it, because it looks impossible. It looks like a superstition to believe that what we say and write, impacts our lives. But I want to tell you something which is even harder to believe: even what you "think" impacts your life also.

I'd like to disclose some important facts that are hard to believe. It is up to you if you want to believe them or not. However, if you like to live more prosperous, you have to believe these facts. If your life is getting better every day, you can make it even better, because it is your right to have a life which is perfect, amazing and outstanding. If your life is what it was used to be in the past 5 years, without any improvement, then you are losing a lot. And if your life isn't what it has to be and is getting worse every day, then you have to do something immediately.

Just start from your thoughts and everything else will get better. Everything will change automatically, if you learn how to feed your thoughts with positive energy. Unfortunately, most people have learned to do the opposite: they feed their thoughts with negativity all the time.

Maybe you can't change the world's economic and political situation. Maybe you can't change the nature and the weather of the area you live in. Maybe you can't change. There are a lot of things you can't change, even if you spend billions of dollars, and even if you have the strongest army in the world.

You are the owner of your mind and thoughts. You can control them. You can program your mind to have good and positive thoughts always. You can do the opposite too. If your mind is full of negative thoughts, they bother you all the time. But you can change them very easily. The negative thoughts have been there for so many years. You are used to them. They come, get amplified and duplicated on their own, because you have allowed them to do that.

Why not having positive thoughts instead of the negative? What advantages do the negative thoughts have for you? The minimum damage they have is that they don't let you enjoy your life. They take away your happiness and tranquility.

But they are more harmful than this. They program your life toward sadness and failure. If you feel you aren't as lucky as what you like to be, it is only because of your thoughts.

So, change your thoughts and then your life will change and it will become what you deserve. You deserve to have a great life, no matter which you are, how old you are, where you are from, and what you have been doing so far.

It is much easier than you can even imagine. You just need to stop thinking and saying the things that have any signs of negativity. Instead, make your mind and talks full of positivity and beauty.

- Never talk about the bad and unpleasant events of your life. If you do that, you are feeding the negativity they have left in your mind, as when you water the weeds. You don't like the weeds to ruin your garden. Similarly, you shouldn't allow the negative thoughts to ruin your mind. When you talk about misery, misfortune, disaster and mischances, you are growing and feeding these harmful weeds in your mind. After a while, they occupy everywhere and they don't allow even one single positive and pleasant thought to come to your mind.

Instead of talking about the bad events and mischances, talk about the funny and pleasant events. Be careful not to allow the negative thoughts to take the control again and make you sad while you are talking about the good things. Laugh as much as you can, when you talk about the good events and stories, and make the listeners laugh also.

Even if there is nobody there to listen to you, talk to yourself. There is nothing wrong with it. I am used to tell jokes to myself and laugh when I am alone. The same jokes that I know for several years are still too funny for me and make me laugh loud when I remember them in my mind.

Make jokes and have fun even if you are you sick and you feel pain. Keep in mind that if you pay attention to anything, you make it stronger. If you pay attention to pains and problems, you make them stronger and you enable them to control you and your life. Instead, pay a lot of attention to good and pleasant things.

Never talk about your pains. Never say you don't feel good, or you feel bad. Always say you are very well and will get better and better every second. Believe me that if you do so, you can defeat even the strongest problems and illnesses. Just try it. It is free. Nobody is going to charge you for the positive thoughts you will have in your mind.

But you always pay the price of your bad thoughts. So, replace them with good thoughts.

-Make the most of any short pleasant moment in your life. If you do so, they expand and duplicate and make your whole life full of happiness, as if you are living in heaven.

Heaven is what you build for yourself. It isn't a special place. Sometimes when you feel so good and you feel you are in paradise, someone who is sitting next to you feels like hell. So, feeling good is all about what you have in your mind. Duplicate good and pleasant thoughts and let them surround you. Enjoy each and every second of the good and joyful events.

-Give positive energy to others. This doesn't waste your positive energy; it amplifies it. You feel much better when you say good and energetic words to others. Conversely, you feel bad when you discourage the others and give them negative energy. Make the others feels good and happy, and you feel better and happier.

Become happy when you see people are happy and successful, and help them become happier and more successful. If so, you attract their happiness and success and the same good things will happen in your life too.

-Always see good things in everything, even if they don't look that good at the beginning. For example, when you see a bad collision which has killed some people, say "thank God! It could be a lot worse than this". Do your best to find at least one good point in any event, even the bad ones?

- Have something good and energetic in anything you say. For example, if you want to ask your friend to bring a cup of tea, say, "please get me a cup of tea my lovely friend".

If your child asks you to buy an expensive toy, don't say, "I can't afford it", because if you do, you will never afford it in future too. Something you say becomes reality, because your mind programs your life according to it. Even something you think is like that. Even if you think that you can't afford something, you really can't afford it in future too, because your mind believes in this thought as a rule that has to be obeyed in your life. Your subconscious believes everything you say and think.

Instead of saying or thinking you can't afford something, challenge your mind to make your life in a way that you become able to afford it soon. You can do this by saying or thinking, "how can I afford this?"

If you say or think like that, then you are pushing your mind to look at what you say, as an address that has to be found. It rules and programs your life toward locating the address, even if you forget about it. Your mind and subconscious always work on the subjects, behind the scene, even when you forget the subjects. Instead of saying "I can't do it", say, "how can I do it"? If you do so, your mind starts working on the project and finds a way to enable you to do it somehow.

- Avoid negative people, places, music's, websites, news, and anything that make you feel bad and negative. Focusing on negativity doesn't take you to a good place. It only takes you down.

Spending your time with negative people and listening to what they say, not only wastes your time, but also ruins your life and future. Avoid people who make you feel bad. Avoid those who don't give you a good sense.

CHAPTER ELEVEN

HOW TO CLEAR NEGATIVE ENERGY FROM YOUR LIFE

When your life gets clouded with negative energy, it can be hard to see through it. It can feel like there's an all-encompassing fog that's never going to clear. But there are unexpected ways to clear negative energy in your life that actually work. Getting rid of the bad vibes in your life is not just an elimination process. Once you've removed the things that don't serve you, you have to rebuild your foundation so that you're a good conductor for positive energy, and so that you don't end up catching that negative energy again when it threatens to boomerang back into your life.

We all go through periods in our lives where the bad outweighs the good, but the key to finding the balance again is finding a hack that works for you. You have to find a method or practice or ritual that helps you put things into perspective. Negative energy can come in the form of people, work stress, or even from within. We all have the ability see things though dim or raised lenses. Here are some practices that you can incorporate into your life when negativity seeps in — they'll help you get back to that positive place you thrive in.

Plant therapy is a real thing. Having living plants around you can help to increase mood and add fresh energy to a space. By nature, plants help to purify the air around them, so think about what they can do for energy; they basically use it up and turn it into something good.

-Get Some Plants

People have been burning sage for centuries as a way to banish negative energy — so there's clearly something to it. As the scent of sage smoke takes over your living space, the prominent smell will give you a very visceral reminder that whatever was there before is now overpowered by a new, positive intention.

-Take a Neutralizing Bath

Adding baking soda and soaking salts to your bath is a great way to neutralize the environment on your skin — literally. The soda and salt combination will reduce inflammation and help restore a healthy pH. These methods are also super helpful in neutralizing yourself mentally. Take a soda and salt soak when you need to reset your vibe.

-Listen to Frequency-Specific Music

Music has been associated with transforming negative energy into positive energy. Listening to sounds at this frequency calms the mind and produces feel-good sensations. If you're sensitive to music, this technique is certainly worth a try.

-Watch a Funny Movie

Laughing breaks up the tension internally by releasing endorphins and also breaks up the energy around you by creating waves in the air. When you're feeling overwhelmed with negative feelings, watch a movie that will make you laugh. Filling your body with feel-good hormones will help you to feel motivated to get rid of negative factors in your life.

-Open All of the Windows

Letting fresh air and sunlight into the room can help to move stagnant energy, change the charge of dull energy, and increase circulation in the room. The sensation of moving air is really helpful when trying to inspire your mind to move on from negative triggers, too.

-Get a Black Tourmaline Crystal

Tourmaline Crystals are believed to be great absorbents of bad energy. Put one on your windowsill and let it collect all of the negativity in your house or carry it with you in your pocket and envision all of the darkness around you dispersing and collecting in the crystal.

-Burn It

Write down all of the behaviors that aren't serving you on a piece of paper and carefully and safely burn the piece of paper. Scoop up the ashes when they're cool and put them in a jar or plastic baggy to dispose of.

-Meditate

Instead of hiding from the negativity that's plaguing you, face it head on. Devote some time to thinking about the negative things in your life and imagine each of those things slipping into a bubble. Pop the bubble with your finger in your mind and let those things go away. Focus on making room for positivity by envisioning what you see as positive.

I don't know about you, but when I look around my house and consider the various items that need to be fixed, it often feels like no money, more problems — especially when payday is a ways off. When I'm feeling that vibe, I call on the genies of the internet to help, because there's no shortage of killer Amazon products that will cut your problems in half, no matter what kind of issue you're having.

Let me just give you one example: You haven't lived until you've tried out the miracle silicone adhesive Sugru. It's just the coolest stuff, because it stays flexible while you're working with it to do everything from fix up floppy shoe soles to mount your artwork to the wall... then overnight, it hardens into a solid, complete with an air-tight, waterproof seal. My favorite use of this amazing substance is to patch my phone charger cords, since I seem to go through a cord every other day. Since the silicone doesn't conduct a current and itself serves as an insulator, it's the perfect answer to make my cords good as new, without worrying and without ordering another gross of them.

CHAPTER TWELVE

POSITIVE ENERGY AND ACHIEVING GOALS

The road to success is not smooth. Making something out of you in our high rising society can be intimidating. With all of the stress that the world puts on becoming successful (interlocking with happy), we can often get discouraged. Keeping a positive mind will set you down the right track to obtain the goals you aspire to achieve. Keeping these 10 thoughts in your mind daily will simultaneously intertwine subtle excitement for the future into your daily life and add confidence into to your future.

-Greatness does not happen overnight

As a society that has grown well-acquainted to the demand for quick access, we often forget that a career is not something that we can receive at a drive-thru. Of course it is frustrating to desire something so badly and feel as if it will take years to obtain it. But, that long wait provides a perfect amount of time for us to exercise our love for what we are looking to achieve. If you continue to strive for the same goal, no matter how long it takes, then you are truly dedicated to what it is that you want. Many give up due to the strenuous working process day after day, but if you keep that light at the end of the tunnel in your vision, you will feel even more satisfied when you reach it.

"Don't let the fear of the time it will take to accomplish something stand in the way of your doing it. The time will pass anyway; we might just as well put that passing time to the best possible use." -Earl Nightingale

-Rejection is inevitable, but it cannot stop you from what you want.

Human beings fall victim to the fear of rejection. Every day, millions of people hesitantly step into the world of business, fashion, medicine, etc. These hopefuls ironically fear what can go wrong rather than what can go right. While the emptiness that rejection leaves us with is like a gash to the heart, it is also a wake-up call. Being turned down from one company does not mean you are not suitable for the job. Being turned away from your top choice of college does not mean you do not have potential or brains. It is up to YOU to take that rejection, toss it to the side, pick yourself up, and go out and try again. Look at it as a bump in the road rather than a dead end. Let rejection build you up, not negatively dictate your future. After all, Walt Disney was fired from a newspaper for "lacking creativity".

-You have far more to offer the world than you think

We are all on this earth for a reason. Sometimes it takes a few ups and downs to find out that reason. It takes trial and error to realize what you can accomplish. Every one of us has the potential to change the world. We all have something within us that were set there at a young age and are waiting to be released. Whether it be a component of our personality that can turn the world into a kinder place, a simple thought that can create extraordinary products, or the drive for success that can form a multi-million dollar company, we all possess a skill. Remind yourself that you have a purpose in life and the world is waiting for you to share it.

-Opportunists set the grounds for society

Those who go out there and make the best of what life has to offer are the happiest. You may get the feeling that there will be no more job openings or internships in your field by the time you are eligible for them. Right? Wrong. We live in a prosperous world that grows with every passing minute. There will always be new opportunities out there. If you mold yourself into one of these kinds of people, you will eventually and surely receive what it is you are looking for. Opportunities are everywhere. Seek and you shall find.

- Risks aren't always bad

Taking your confidence and turning it I to risk taking is an excellent attribute. Risks are scary to most, for it takes one out of their comfort zone. This being said, stepping out of tor comfort zone is a step in the right direction. Life begins when you remove yourself from what you're used to. Tell yourself that it's okay to enter new territories! Travel. Take chances. Do something that you're scared of. Set up a job interview with a prestigious company. Put yourself out there without fear.

- Pick one present you want to reward yourself with when you reach a milestone

The road to your future doesn't have to be strictly stiff business. Giving yourself leeway for pleasure will help you stay on track. Set smaller goals on the road to your large goal. When you land an internship, treat yourself to a nice pair of shoes. When you get a raise, reward yourself with that watch you've always wanted. Praising yourself for your accomplishments will help you stay focused to keep working as hard as you can. Remember that you are a human and humans need self-fulfillment to progress.

- Support System

If you're lucky enough to have a single person that believes in all that you are, you're lucky enough. Not every successful person was fortunate enough to have a handful of people that supported them along every failure and triumph. If you have a close knit group of people you can rely on to boost you up when you've reached your lowest, you should thank them often. You may feel alone along the road to success, but remember those that are rooting for you. You can find this support in parents, relatives, friends, teachers, etc. Don't take them for granted. They are the ones who will be by your side when you start from the bottom and when you reach the top.

- You are already halfway to your goal just by dreaming of it- now get out and do it!

There are millions of people that lack any ambition. Those that do not strive for any sort of success are the ones who will not make it nearly as far in life as you will. By experiencing failures and rejection, you are steps ahead of those who don't even try. Remind yourself that you are already closer to reaching your dreams and goals just by having the courage to dream at all!

-Remove "can't" from your vocabulary.

It is one of the most cliché sayings but holds much truth. When you restrict yourself from something because you think that you "can't" do it, you are only withholding great potential from the matter. You CAN do it. We all are capable of greatness. Recite "I CAN do this" to yourself 5 times when in doubt.

-You are capable of anything and everything.

When you get up in the morning, don't rush to get a cup of coffee. Rather look in the mirror and remind yourself that today is another day to set forth towards your goals. You have the ability and resources you need. Release any negative thoughts and remember that you are a strong person who can satisfy your innermost desires as soon as you make the first step to do so. You have strength, courage, wisdom, and individually thrust upon you. Make it count.

Everywhere you turn there are products claiming to be the best? Even savvy shoppers can get confused and spend way too much on tools and devices that turn out to be duds — but this list of Amazon products with five-star ratings cuts out the possibility of wasting your money on beauty products and kitchen tools that'll end up in the trash. These products have won over thousands of happy Amazon customers, and there's a good chance they'll become your new favorites, too.

Maybe you're searching for a ski mask that will actually make blackheads disappear instead of just smelling nice. Or perhaps you've decided you're never letting another nasty cleaning chemical into your life again, but are struggling to find genius cleaning inventions that will rid your house of dust without kicking up your allergies. Whether you desperately need a back massage but can't afford to hire a personal masseuse, or you really want to find a way to wash sharp knives without slicing your finger, this list includes products that do everything and have the highest ratings possible to prove it.

If you looked up "cult classic masks," this carbonated bubble clay mask would be right up at the top of the list. First of all, it's a fun science experiment come to life: apply the charcoal powder, mud, and clay mask and wait five minutes for it to bubble up right on your skin. More importantly, it works. Reviewers say consistent use of this Korean beauty mask rids skin of excess oil and prevents and treats blackheads. It cleans skin, exfoliates, and banishes blackheads from your life.

There are a ton of great flat irons out there, but they aren't all safe for all hair types. This titanium flat iron is made with far-infrared technology that actually hydrates your hair while you're using it and its heat range is so wide it works on all hair types and textures — and is even safe for hair that's damaged. The 1-inch plate is perfect for short hair and bang but can be effective on all hair lengths. It also has an auto-shutoff feature that turns the device off after 90 minutes, so you'll never panic on your commute and obsess all day about whether you unplugged your iron.

This portable charger combines the best of both charger worlds; it's lightweight and won't make a dent in your pocket or purse. But it's also powerful and can deliver over three charges for an iPhone 6sor over two for a Galaxy S6. The safety system ensures your devices will be protected while charging, which is a relief, and there's even a power button on the charger that shows you (via blue LED light) how much power is left on your device.

This stress relief essential oils blend is the most calming, soothing, stress-relieving aromatherapy treatment imaginable. It's made with 100 percent pure therapeutic-grade ylang ylang, grapefruit, patchouli, and blood orange, and is packaged in a bottle that comes with a convenient dropper cap. Even long-time aromatherapy devotees say there's something special about this blend: "I have used essential oils for at least 15 years and this to me has the best aroma and it works to calm me down and relax".

"These are magic cloths - they hold water like a sponge without leaking.," Writes one of the many obsessed fans of these cleaning cloths. These microfiber cleaning cloths are a big step up from old towels — and are all you need to get rid of dust and grossness without scratching up your furniture, and they hold eight times their weight in water. You'll get 48 cloths in a pack and each can be washed and reused hundreds of times.

This eye pillow blocks out annoying light from street lamps or the morning sun on a weekend when you want to sleep in, but that's not its only magic trick. It doubles as a compression pain relief mask that can reduce headache and sinus pain and even help with puffy eyes. It conforms to your face without squeezing you too tight, and is made from breathable cotton and ergo Beads that provide a gentle massage. Pop it in the freezer for a few minutes when you want cooling relief.

CHAPTER THIRTEEN

HISTORY OF POSITIVE ENERGY

During the second half of the 19th century and the early part of the 20th, psychology was concerned with curing mental disorders, such as schizophrenia and human complexes of various kinds (inferiority, power, electra, oedipus, other). And why not? There has always been, and will perhaps always be, a significant incidence of mental illness in all communities, irrespective of race or religion, caste or creed.

The attempt of psychologists to cure these ailments was quite natural and laudable, and the work of early psychologists, such as Sigmund Freud, Adler, and Carl Jung was indeed very effective. (Note: It must be added here that of these 3 pioneers, the big 3 of Vienna as they were called, Carl Jung was perhaps the earliest psychologist to recognize, and be troubled by, psychology's negative focus.

Over time, this disease focus pushed psychology towards the dark recesses of the human mind and away from the deeper well-springs of human energy and potential. As highlighted by Martin Seligman, in his 2008 TED talk on Positive Psychology, the negative focus of psychology resulted in three major drawbacks for the field:

Firstly, psychologists became victimologists and pathologizers (they forgot that people make choices, and have responsibility.

Secondly, they forgot about improving normal lives and high talent (the mission to make relatively untroubled people happier, more fulfilled, more productive).

Thirdly, in their rush to repair damage, it never occurred to them to develop interventions to make people happier.

B. F. Skinner of Harvard University was the originator, along with John B. Watson and Ivan Pavlov, of the behavioral approach in psychology. Skinner believed that free will was an illusion, and human behavior was largely dependent on the consequences of our previous actions. If a particular behavior attracted the right type of reinforcement, it had a high probability of being repeated, and if, on the other hand, the behavior resulted in punishment, it had a good chance of not being repeated.

Skinner believed that, given the right structure of rewards and punishments, human behavior could be totally modified, in an almost mechanical sense.This theory undoubtedly has a lot of merits, particularly the idea of operant conditioning, with its relevance to the workplace and the home, in terms of influencing and eliciting desired behavior, through a well-conceived reward system. But Skinner's total rejection of free will is still disturbing.

It goes against all that human history stands for – the ultimate and enduring triumph of the human spirit against overwhelming odds. Also, his idea of behavior modification, meaning the manipulation of behavior through properly structured rewards, is open to gross abuse by autocrats and dictators, in terms of oppressing their subjects. And not just in society at large, but in the workplace as well. J E R Staddon and Noam Choksy were among Skinner's major critics (Staddon, J., 1995; Chomsky, Noam 1959).

Criticisms of his theory notwithstanding, Skinner stands tall — a brilliant Harvard psychologist and prolific writer, with 21 books and 180 articles to his credit, and whom in a 2002 survey, was voted the most influential psychologist of the twentieth century (Haggbloom, Steven J. et. al, 200 .)

This wave is known for its two major strands of thought – existentialist psychology (Soren Kierkegaard, Jean Paul Sartre) and humanistic psychology (Abraham Maslow and Carl Rogers.)

According to Sartre, every human being is responsible for working out his identity and his life's meaning, through the interaction between himself and his surroundings. No one else can do it for him, least of all a non-existent God.

For this reason, meaning is something truly unique to each person – separate and independent (Jean-Paul Sartre, 1946.)

One cannot quarrel with this strand of thought, particularly the responsibility of the individual for his own destiny, but the underlying atheism is dampening. What about people who cannot find their identity and their life's meaning on their own?

Uncontrollable anxiety would be inevitable, particularly in the absence of faith in a supernatural being, an idea rejected by existentialism. This anxiety is recognized in psychotherapy as "existential anxiety" and has been of major therapeutic concern of many leading psychologists, particularly Victor Frankl, the originator of logo-therapy.

There is a considerable divergence of views on the question of "What is life's meaning?" and, clearly, each one needs to work it out for himself, with his own unique experience and surroundings. Here is a very thoughtful quote from Kierkegaard, arguably the earliest exponent of existentialist.

"What I really need is to get clear about what I must do, not what I must know, except insofar as knowledge must precede every act. What matters is to find a purpose, to see what it really is that God wills that I shall do; the crucial thing is to find a truth which is truth for me, to find the idea for which I am willing to live and die. (…) I certainly do not deny that I still accept an imperative of knowledge and that through it men may be influenced, but then it must come alive in me and this is what I now recognize as the most important of all" (Kierkegaard, Soren, 1962.)

The humanistic movement was about adding a holistic dimension to psychology. Humanistic psychologists believed that our behavior was determined by our perception of the world around us and its meanings, we are not the sole product of our environment or biochemistry, and that we are internally influenced and motivated to fulfill our human potential.

Humanistic psychology emphasizes the inherent human drive towards self-actualization, the process of realizing and expressing one's own capabilities and creativity. This approach rose to prominence in the mid-20th century in response to the limitations of the disease model in fulfilling the human desire for actualization and a life of meaning (Benjafield, John G., 2010).

As already pointed out earlier in this article, positive psychology is psychology with a positive orientation, concerned with authentic happiness and the good life. Humanistic psychologist Abraham Maslow maintained that psychology itself does not have an accurate understanding of human potential and that the field tends to raise the proverbial bar not high enough with respect to maximum attainment.

He wrote "The science of psychology has been far more successful on the negative than on the positive side; it has revealed to us much about man's shortcomings, his illnesses, his sins, but little about his potentialities, his virtues, his achievable aspirations, or his full psychological height. It is as if psychology had voluntarily restricted itself to only half its rightful jurisdiction, and that the darker, meaner half".

While the previous waves of psychology focused on human flaws, overcoming deficiencies, avoiding pain, and escape from unhappiness, positive psychology, focuses on well-being, contentment, excitement, cheerfulness, the pursuit of happiness and meaning in life.

The humanistic movement wanted to look at what drives us to want to grow and achieve fulfillment, however, even though their conceptual ideas of human nature did influence the development of positive psychology, they are separate. While the humanistic approach used more qualitative methods, positive psychology is developing a more scientific epistemology of understanding human beings.Psychology may, at last, be converging into the quintessence of the world's great religions. It may finally be discovering that the key to human evolution lies in a fine blend of the mind and the spirit.

In 1998, Martin Seligman was elected President of the American Psychological Association and it was then that Positive Psychology became the theme of his term as president. He is widely seen as the father of contemporary positive psychology (About Education, 2013).

However, while most people see Seligman as the face of Positive Psychology, he didn't start the field alone and was not the first 'positive psychologist'. In fact, there have been many influencers which have contributed to this new era of psychology.

- William James

James was a philosopher, physician, and psychologist and he was the first educator to offer a psychology course in the United States. He argued that in order to thoroughly study a person's optimal functioning, one has to take in how they personally experience something, otherwise known as subjective experience.

He also saw the importance in combining both positivistic and phonological methodology, which is what many now refer to as "radical empiricism", because he was interested in what was objective and observable. Despite this, many consider James to be America's "first positive psychologist" (Froh, 2004) because of his deep interest in the subjectivity of a person, and believed that "objectivity is based on intense subjectivity" (2004).

-Abraham Maslow

Abraham Maslow While the entire 3rd Wave of Humanistic Psychology played a vital role in providing

Positive Psychology with foundational concepts, there was no greater influence from the approach then Abraham Maslow.

In fact, the term "positive psychology" was first coined by Maslow, in his 1954 book "Motivation and Personality". Maslow did not like how psychology concerned itself mostly with disorder and dysfunction, arguing that it did not have an accurate understanding of human potential. He emphasized how psychology successfully shows our negative side by revealing much about our illnesses and shortcomings, but not enough on our virtues or aspirations.

-Martin Seligman

Seligman is an American Psychologist, educator, and author of self-help books. He is famous for his experiments and theory of learned helplessness is for being the founder of Positive Psychology.

His work in learned helplessness and pessimistic attitudes garnered an interest in optimism, which cued his work with Christopher Peterson (mentioned below) to create a positive side to the Diagnostic and Statistical Manual of Mental Disorders (DSM). In their research, they looked at different cultures over time to create a list of virtues that are highly valued and included it in their Character Strengths and Virtues section in the DSM: wisdom/knowledge, courage, transcendence, justice, humanity, and temperance.

In 1996, he was elected President of the American Psychological Association and the central theme he chose for his term as president was positive psychology. He wanted mental health to be more than just the "absence of illness" and was determined to bring psychology to a new era that focused on what makes people feel happy and fulfilled. Today he is the director of the Positive Psychology Center at the University of Pennsylvania.

- Mihaly Czikszentmihalyi

Czikszentmihalyi was born in Hungary in 1934, and like many other people of that time, he was deeply affected by the Second World War. He was stripped from his family and friends as a child and was put in an Italian prison and it was there he had his first idea of working with flow and optimal experience .

He had an affinity for painting, noting that the act of creating was sometimes more important than the finished work itself. Which cued his fascination with what he called the flow state and he made it his life's work to scientifically identify the different methods through which one could achieve such a state. His studies and findings gained much popular interested that today he is considered as one of the founders of positive psychology.

- Christopher Peterson

Christopher Peterson was the professor of Psychology at the University of Michigan and the former chair of the

Clinical Psychology department. He was the co-author of Character Strengths and Virtues with Seligman and is noted for his work in the study of optimism, hope, character, and well-being and his important findings make him one of the founders of Positive Psychology for helping to bring Psychology into this new era.

The following positive psychology researchers deserve a special mention. However, there are so many positive psychology researchers whose work is shaping the future of positive psychology that can't all be mentioned in this article. Check out our full list of Positive Psychology Researchers .

-Albert Bandura

Albert Bandura's self-efficacy theory originated from his Social-Cognitive theory. It relates to a person's perception of their ability to reach a goal and the belief that one is capable of performing it in a certain way in order to reach them. This concept has served to be of great impotence and use in positive psychology.

-Donald Clifton

Seligman stated that Clifton followed a similar path that he did when he came up with Strengths-based psychology. He studied successful individuals and wanted to know what they did right to achieve top performance.

His work gave employers solid recommendations on how to find a fulfilling career that is suitable for them. He was honored in 2002 by the American Psychological Association with a Presidential Commendation as the Father of Strengths-based Psychology and he has been called the "grandfather of Positive Psychology")

-Deci and Ryan

The Theory of human motivation known as Self Determination Theory was developed in 2000 by Edward L. Deci, professor in the Department of Clinical and Social Sciences and Richard at the University of Rochester, New

York and Richard M. Ryan, clinical psychologist and Professor at the Institute for Positive Psychology and Education at the Australian Catholic University in Sydney, Australia.

Their grounding work on Self-Determination Theory updated the hierarchy of needs that was originally identified by Abraham Maslow and found that human motivation is founded in three major needs: autonomy, competence, and relatedness (connecting to other people) .

-Ed Diener

Dr. Ed Diener, aka "Dr. Happiness", is a leading researcher in PP who coined the term "Subjective well-being" as the aspect of happiness that can be measured scientifically. His argument that there is a strong genetic component to happiness has led to a huge amount of data studying the internal and external conditions of happiness and how one can change it. He even researched the relationship between income and well-being, as well as cultural influences on well-being. His publications have been cited over 98,000 times and his fundamental research on the subject is what earned him his nickname. He has worked with researchers Daniel Kahneman and Martin Seligman and is a senior scientist for The Gallup Organization.

-Carol Dweck

Dweck conducted research on the notion of growth vs. fixed mindset. It has been used with parents, teams, students, entrepreneurs, and business leaders. It is a positive psychology tool that is used widely and praised highly, bringing people more interest to the world of positive psychology.

-Barbara Fredrickson

World-renowned author and researcher, Fredrickson made her first contribution to positive psychology research with her theory on positive emotions, The Broaden and Build Theory, which proposes the idea that positive emotions are able to broaden people's minds resulting in resources for helping cope and experience well-being and resilience in times of adversity. Since then Fredrickson has done extensive research and produced 2 books. She currently acts as the Director of the Positive Emotions and Psychophysiology Laboratory, University of North Carolina at Chapel Hill .

CHAPTER FOURTEEN
POSITIVE ENERGY AND MEDICINE

Energy is the life force. Keep your life force healthy and it keeps you healthy. Energy Medicine gets your energies into harmony and balance. If you are sick or sad, shifting your energies feels good. Balancing your energies balances your body's chemistry, regulates your hormones, helps you feel good, and helps you think better.

When you care for your body's invisible energies, your cells become a cell's version of happy, all the systems in your body start to hum in tune, and your heart begins to sing. Energy Medicine has been called the medicine of the future, but it empowers you NOW to adapt to the challenges of the 21st century and to thrive within them.

How Does Energy Medicine Work?

Energy Medicine uses techniques from time-honored traditions such as acupuncture, yoga, kinesiology, and Qigong. Flow, balance, and harmony can be noninvasively restored and maintained within an energy system by:

- Tapping, massaging, pinching, twisting, or connecting specific energy points on the skin;

- Tracing or swirling the hand over the skin along specific energy pathways;

- Exercises or postures designed for specific energetic effects;

- Focused use of the mind to move specific energies and/or by surrounding an area with healing energies.

Energy Medicine and conventional medicine can work in a wonderful harmony. Conventional Western medicine, at its foundation, focuses on the biochemistry of cells, tissue, and organs. On the other hand, Energy Medicine at its foundation focuses on the energy fields of the body that organize and control the growth and repair of cells, tissue, and organs.

To maintain vibrant health, the body needs its energies to:

- Move and have space to continue to move — energies may become blocked due to toxins, muscular or other constrictions, prolonged stress, or interference from other energies.

- Move in specific patterns — generally in harmony with the physical structures and functions that the energies animate and support. "Flow follows function."

- Cross-over — at all levels; from the micro-level of the double helix of DNA, to the macro-level where the left side of the brain controls the right side of the body and the right side controls the left.

- Maintain a balance with other energies — the energies may lose their natural balance due to prolonged stress or other conditions that keep specific energy systems in a survival mode.

Conversely, when the body is not healthy, corresponding disturbances in its energies can be identified and treated. By changing impaired energy patterns, we improve the vitality of organs, cells, and psyche through the most efficient, least invasive means.

Healthcare Systems Could Benefit By Embracing Energy Medicine More Fully. Medical technology has become so sophisticated that routine procedures result in what would have seemed like miracles a few decades ago. Yet, as Michael Moore powerfully demonstrated in his documentary, Sicko, the system is breaking down. The Western health care system isn't effective because it isn't preventative. We don't step in until after the person is already sick.

Energy Medicine, on the other hand, gives everyone tools that will keep them healthy as a first line for healing. Energy Medicine traces back to venerable healing and spiritual systems. In some provinces of ancient China, for example, you paid the doctor when you were well. You didn't pay if you got sick because the doctor had failed to keep your energies — and therefore your physical body — in a healthy state. The doctor then had to work very hard to get your energies back into harmony so that your body would follow those energies back into health.

While it is not likely that your local hospital will agree to this arrangement, the principle is well worth incorporating. Changes in the physical body are shaped by and follow changes in energy fields and flows. Christiane Northrup, MD, known for her New York Times bestselling books and many appearances on Oprah, sums up how Energy Medicine can inform and complement conventional medicine.

In the medicine of the future, as I envision it, working with the patient's energy field will be the first intervention. Surgery will be a last resort. Drugs will be a last resort. They will still have their place, but shifting the energy patterns that caused the disease will be the first line of treatment. And before that, teaching people how to keep their energies in healthy patterns will be as much a part of physical hygiene as flossing or exercise.

Why the Rise of Energy Medicine?

Here are the reasons why people (including many physicians and health care professionals) are increasingly using Energy Medicine:

• Balance the body's energies before an invasive medical procedure, prepares the body for a healing outcome, leaves the patient more confident and relaxed, and makes the procedure more likely to succeed;

• Balance the body's energies after an invasive medical procedure to minimize side effects and enhance recovery;

• Prevent or help overcome challenging illnesses;

- Energy Medicine is simple, pleasant, and non-invasive;

- The body's energy fields can be restabilized on a regular basis through simple, cost-effective practices;

- Energy Medicine has no adverse side effects;

- Patients are increasingly asking for alternative preventative care and healing methods.

You don't have to be a gifted healer to start using energy medicine to keep your life force healthy. Keep your energies humming and your body will be functioning at its best.

Reasons Energy Medicine Is the Best Medicine

What if I told you there is a way to heal yourself of all types of distress without pills or hospital stays or side effects or surgeries? A painless procedure that has virtually zero recovery time? You'd probably say, "Sign me up!"

Whether your issues are mental, physical, emotional, or spiritual, energy medicine can address the root causes of the illness and heal you completely without touching a scalpel to your skin or even taking any invasive medical tests! As an energy healer and spiritual teacher, I've seen energy healing work its magic on tens of thousands of people who walk away from sessions with me healed and restored, with renewed energy and lightness to their body. From a broken leg to a broken heart, energy healing can help you recover from your condition, and better yet, teach you how to heal yourself.

What Exactly Is Energy Medicine?

Interest in energy medicine is on the rise. Decades ago when I started studying and practicing energy healing, people thought it was pretty "out there" stuff. But over the years, energy medicine has become more and more common, and has gained more respect from the general public. These days, many people know someone who was healed by an energy healer, or have at least heard of this thing called energy medicine.

Energy exists all around us, on multiple levels or fields, and interpenetrates every living and non-living thing on this planet and beyond. Humans have their own personal energy fields that mirror what is happening in the body, which means that making changes in your personal energy field can make changes in your physical body. Likewise, changes in your body can affect your energy field. This is how energy medicine works: by tapping into the unified field of all energy, an energy healer manipulates your energy field to heal both your energy and, consequently, your body

One of the ways you can test the health of your energy field is through the chakras. Your chakras are focal points of energy in your body that reflect the movement of energy in your field. An energy healer can sense where there are blockages or distortions in your chakras, and therefore your energy flow, and then clear the negative energy away so your chakra can function freely as it's supposed to. This energy exchange that keeps you nourished is vital to all aspects of your health. This is why it's important to keep your body and energy field free and clear of negative energy. Meditation, journaling, and staying grounded in nature are all good ways to begin the practice of clearing your chakras and allowing energy medicine to begin its healing process. Whether you are seeking healing for yourself or a loved one, read these three reasons to give energy medicine a try. It just might save your life.

. Energy medicine heals your whole being.

Your mind, body, spirit, and emotions are like threads weaved together into the tapestry of you. If you pull at one string, the whole structure unravels. If you only treat the physical symptoms of a condition or illness, you've left the rest of the person out of the equation. Emotional and spiritual pain can cause physical distress. Like the closed heart chakra contributing to high cholesterol, I've seen time and time again the very real effects that feelings can have on the body.

Each aspect of your being affects the other aspects, and traditional western medicine has a one-track mind: physical body issues only. It fails to treat the emotional, spiritual, or mental components of illness, which means it fails to treat the totality of the sick person. Western medicine is good at saving lives when the situation is acute, but energy medicine can prevent a condition from getting that far in the first place.

. Energy medicine can prevent physical symptoms from developing.

One of the main advantages of energy medicine is its amazing ability to detect illnesses or conditions that are brewing in your energy field long before any symptoms appear in the body. Distortions in your chakras can be revealed through taking healing courses or working with an energy healer, and when they are caught early enough, you may not develop any physical ailments related to that distortion at all. Imagine having your sickness healed before you really even felt sick!

Most medical practitioners would agree that prevention is always the best medicine. Meditation, journaling, and healing courses are all tools to keep you on track, but if your health does become threatened, wouldn't you want to know about it as soon as possible? Energy medicine allows for the soonest possible detection.

. Zero negative side effects and almost zero recovery time.

Energy medicine is a painless procedure. Sometimes patients feel warmth surrounding a physical healing and others find that an emotional healing will release a slew of tears. But there are no invasive procedures performed by faceless doctors in brightly lit and sterile hospital rooms, no stitches or crutches, no weeks of recovery time or tons of prescription pain pills.

Energy medicine works with the body to heal from within, so the physical recovery is minimal. Some patients feel immediately better and walk away from an energy healer like they've got clouds under their feet. Others feel a shift that grows and develops over the next few hours or days until the effects have fully unfolded. Either way, you should try to take it easy after an energy healing session, and be sure to drink plenty of water. But that is the extent of the "post-op procedure" and there's no need to deal with insurance.

Some of the side effects of energy medicine that you might encounter include feelings of joy and relief, a lightened spirit, a sense of freedom, an emotional rebirth, a physical improvement, or any number of positive transitions in your mental, spiritual, physical, or emotional well-being.

If you would like to learn more about energy medicine and its boundless healing potential, check out my Hay House Life-force Energy Healing Online Course, a twelve week program designed to teach you how to heal yourself and others, and certifies you to be an official energy healer!

CHAPTER FIFTEEN

POSITIVE ENERGY AND CHILD

Positive vibes help children to grow-up into healthy, happy and well balanced individuals. Have a quick look at some tips for attracting positive energy around your children.

Positive Energy or Chi as it is called in Feng Shui is responsible for attracting good fortune, positive events and wish fulfillment in life. As a parent it is perfectly natural that you would want your kids to have the best that life can offer them. With a little effort and by following some simple tricks you will be able to attract positive energy in the life of your children.

De-Clutter

Positive energy is negatively affected by clutter and congestion. If you want to fill your kid's lives with positive energy then your first job should be to remove all clutter from your home. Set up a weekly de-cluttering day in which you throw, give or recycle all unnecessary and unwanted stuff that keeps piling up at home. If your kids are too young to clean up after themselves then make sure that you do this for them. The best thing is that your kids will learn the skill of neatness from you.

Music

Music is one of the best therapeutic forces in the world and it has an immensely positive effect on the mind as well as body. According to research; listening to music can reduce stress, frustration and the negative forces of the mind. Listening to the right kind of music can also increase concentration, focus and physical wellbeing. Make sure that your children develop a taste for listening to fine musical compositions by Masters like Beethoven and Mozart as this will help fill their lives with positive energy.

Gardening

Being around living growing things has a very positive regenerative effect on the minds of children. It has been scientifically proved that children who were exposed to activities like gardening from their early years develop a more humane and kind approach as adults.

Gardening teaches kids the skill and patience needed to nurture life and watching plants and herbs grow soothes their mind. Gardening will also wean your kids away from detrimental activities like too many video games and unsuitable TV content.

Practice Gratitude

Gratitude brings about a happy content feeling in the mind and this in turn attracts positive energy. Teach your kids the art of gratefulness and they are sure to mature into healthy content adults. You need to sit down with you children once a week and list down all the things that you are grateful about. Then ask your kids to make their own lists and read them aloud. This activity will immediately generate a positive vibe in the minds of your children as they realize the many things that are blessed with.

Shed All Negative Thoughts

Anger, resentment, jealousy and the desire to control others are just some of the negative forces that suck away the positive energy out of your kid's lives. You need to teach your children to let go off their negative feelings so that more space is available for the positive energy to

work its wonders. Negative thoughts are difficult to eradicate completely so what you can do is to teach your kids to counsel themselves by self-motivation whenever their minds are hit by negative urges.

Spread Love

Love is the antidote to all negative elements. Spread love throughout your home by warm and friendly conversation, hugs and kisses and verbal demonstration of your love as a family unit. The knowledge that parents love them and dote on them can be the biggest support for a child. A mind which receives and acknowledges love will automatically shed off its negativity to morph into a positive and happy frame.

REFERENCES

- R. Schoen and S.-T. Yau, "On the proof of the positive mass conjecture in general relativity", *Commun. Math. Phys.* 65, 45 (1979).

- G. T. Horowitz and M. J. Perry, "Gravitational mass cannot become negative", Phys. Rev. Lett. 48, 371 (1982).

- G. T. Horowitz and M. J. Perry, "Gravitational mass cannot become negative", Phys. Rev. Lett. 48, 371 (1982).

- 11 Ways to Bring Positive Energy into Your Life, https://blog.mindvalley.com/positiveenergy/?utm_sou rce=google.

- 13 Ways to Project Positive Energy, By Rebecca Wojno, https://www.happify.com/hd/13-proven-ways-to-project-positive-energy/

- 20 Simple Ways to Bring Positive Energy into Your Life Right Now, https://www.lifehack.org/569466/how-regain-your-positive-energy-when-things-are-getting-tough.

- How to Use Positive Energy to Succeed, By Christina Des Marais https://www.inc.com/christina-desmarais/how-to-use-positive-energy-to-succeed.html.

- E. Witten, "A new proof of the positive energy theorem", Commun. Math. Phys. 80, 381 (1981).

- M. Ludvigsen and J. A. G. Vickers, "The positivity of the Bondi mass", J. Phys. A 14, L389 (1981).

- https://www.discogs.com/Alpha-Blondy-The-Solar-System-Positive-Energy/master/1174603.

- https://www.amazon.com/Positive-Energy-Alpha-Blondy-System/dp/B00VMRNG5Q.

- Alan Guth The Inflationary Universe: The Quest for a New Theory of Cosmic Origins (1997), Random House, ISBN 0-224-04448-6 Appendix A: Gravitational Energy demonstrates the negativity of gravitational energy.

- Stephen Hawking; The Grand Design, 2010, Page 180.

- Everett, Allen; Roman, Thomas (2012). Time Travel and Warp Drives. University of Chicago Press. p. 167. ISBN 0-226-22498-8.